A Christmas Journey

SUSIE POOLE

Thanks to Jonnie B, Malcolm Down, Phil Grundy, Julie Clayden, Jo Poole,
Peter and Veronica Batsford, John Nicholson and Mum

A Christmas Journey

Susie Poole

What an exciting time of year! We're getting ready for Christmas.

The streets look so beautiful as they sparkle with colored lights. Soon our Christmas tree will glow cheerily through the window, heavy with ornaments, ribbons and tinsel.

Have you seen Santa Claus waving through the shop windows? I love to pat his rosy cheeks and snuggle up on his red, velvet lap, warm and cosy. I always smile at him sweetly, hoping for a present or two.

At home, we light pretty candles and put them on a high shelf where they light up the whole room. As the flames dance this way and that, we remember the time, long ago, when God sent his Christmas light into the world. God loves light. He always has. It was the first thing he had ever made and it was very, very good.

Here our Christmas journey begins.

When everything was dark, empty and cold,
God decided that the time had come to create a
beautiful world, full of his wonderful light. So he used
his magnificent voice and for the first time ever,
spoke the words,

'Let there be light.'

And there was.

God pushed the light and dark apart and in doing so,
made the first day.

Now God had many creation ideas buzzing around in his
head and so he made the sky, the sea, and the islands.
Then filled them up with every kind of living thing,
big and small: from the most enormous elephant
to the teeny-weeniest terrapin.

God had nearly finished making his beautiful, brand new world when he said. . .

'Let us make someone extra special, someone who will be just like us.'

'Let us make a person!'

And so He did.

He made a man called Adam and he was handsome; too handsome to live alone. So God gave him a lovely woman to be his wife, called Eve.

God made Eden, a beautiful garden for Adam and Eve to live in. There they ruled over the animals, ate delicious food and, best of all, walked and talked with their wonderful daddy, God.

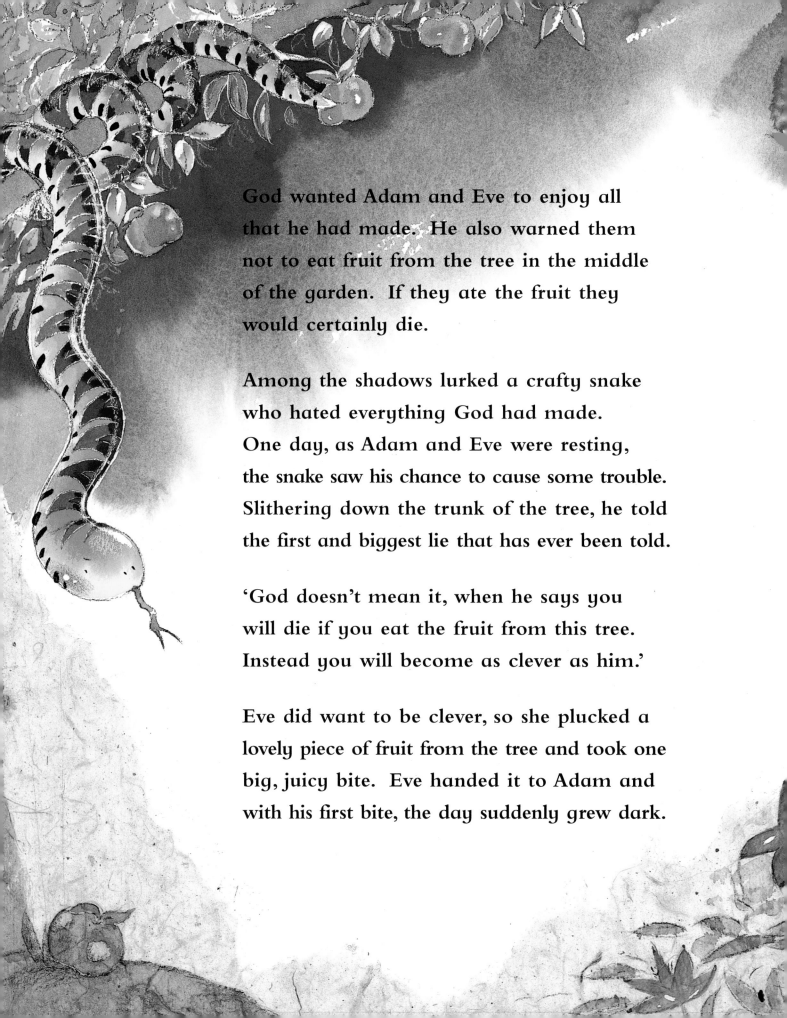

God wanted Adam and Eve to enjoy all
that he had made. He also warned them
not to eat fruit from the tree in the middle
of the garden. If they ate the fruit they
would certainly die.

Among the shadows lurked a crafty snake
who hated everything God had made.
One day, as Adam and Eve were resting,
the snake saw his chance to cause some trouble.
Slithering down the trunk of the tree, he told
the first and biggest lie that has ever been told.

'God doesn't mean it, when he says you
will die if you eat the fruit from this tree.
Instead you will become as clever as him.'

Eve did want to be clever, so she plucked a
lovely piece of fruit from the tree and took one
big, juicy bite. Eve handed it to Adam and
with his first bite, the day suddenly grew dark.

They knew they had made a big mistake.

Adam and Eve hoped God would not see
what they had done. But it was too late.
With a sad and heavy heart, God had no
choice but to send them away from the
garden, forever.

Adam and Eve cried.

God cried too.

Adam and Eve had disobeyed God. Everything had changed. Away from the garden, they felt cold. So God made them clothes from animal skins to keep them warm.

Adam and Eve had lots of children. Soon they filled the whole earth. They were full of hate and forgot what it was like to have God's wonderful light living inside them. But God still loved them. He had a plan to bring his light back.

God's plan was like a big jigsaw puzzle. As the years passed, he would give little puzzle pieces to men and women who loved him and longed for his light. He gave one piece to a man called Isaiah. This is what God said to him . . .

"People who are walking in the darkness will see a great light, for a child will be born and he will rule the world, bringing peace, fairness and goodness. . . . He will be called "God with Us"."

Many people tried to guess what the puzzle pieces meant.
Some put the pieces together in the wrong order.
Nobody could agree on what God would do.

Zechariah and Elizabeth were an old couple who spent
their lives loving God, longing for his light and praying
for a family. But now they were too old to have a baby.

Zechariah was a priest who served in the temple
in Jerusalem. While on special duty one day, a miracle
began to grow in the dark temple corners.
A bright light shone all around him and there,
in the middle of it, stood a mighty
gleaming angel called Gabriel.

'Greetings!' said the angel. 'God is
going to give you the son you have
always longed for. You will call him
John and he will have the job of
getting people ready to meet
the 'Savior King', the one
who will bring God's light
back into the world.'

Zechariah was amazed. Perhaps that is
why he doubted the angel's words.
But asking the angel whether he had
mixed up his message was a big mistake.

To prove it was true, the angel took
away Zechariah's voice until the day
the baby was born.

Zechariah and Elizabeth had
plenty to do. They wanted to
be ready for this special baby.

In the village of Nazareth, their young relative, Mary, was making preparations of her own. She was soon to be married to Joseph.

As Mary swept and baked, washed and mended, she sang 'thank you' songs to God. She had no idea that God had been looking everywhere for a heart as beautiful as hers. He had chosen her for a very special task.

That night, heaven hushed its singing and the angel Gabriel visited earth once more, to bring God's most important message to Mary.

'You are very special and God is with you' whispered Gabriel. 'He will surprise you with a son and you will call him Jesus. His Kingdom will rule for ever and ever. The spirit of God will rest on you so that your baby will be called the perfect Son of God'.

Gabriel told Mary all about Zechariah and Elizabeth's miracle baby.

'You see' he smiled, 'nothing is impossible for God!'

'Yes' replied Mary, 'I do see. Let everything you have said happen to me'.

The next day, Mary quickly packed her things and joined some travelers journeying to Elizabeth's village, in Judea.

'Is anybody home?', called Mary. At the sound of these words, the baby in Elizabeth's tummy leapt and wriggled. This baby knew that somebody special had arrived.

Elizabeth was so happy that she laughed, cried and sang a new song . . .

'You are so blessed,
More blessed than the rest,
Your baby has caused me to sing.
But who am I that you should come
To me, with such great news to bring.'

Mary sang too . . .

'I'm dancing and singing the song of my God,
I'm happy as happy could be.
God looked through earth for a woman to bless,
And look who he chose, he chose me.
The weak will be strong,
The poor will be rich,
The proud won't be proud any more.
He promised to give us this wonderful gift,
Now it's waiting for us at the door.'

While the baby was growing in Elizabeth's tummy,
Zechariah was unable to speak. So when the baby
was born and let out his first cry, Zechariah let out
a cry too.

When the time came to name the baby, Zechariah
remembered what the angel Gabriel had said and
called him John.

'God you are fantastic,' cried Zechariah.
'You are giving us one who will show us your light in
the darkness. You have remembered your promises
to us. And my son John has arrived first to make sure
that everyone is ready to meet the one who is coming.'

It was time to leave. With wonder in her heart,
Mary kissed baby John, said goodbye and began
the long journey home.

Now that Mary had returned to Nazareth it was time to tell Joseph about all the amazing events that had taken place. First she told him about Zechariah and Elizabeth's baby. Joseph thought this was wonderful news and he clapped with joy. Then Mary told Joseph about her baby.

This, Joseph decided, was not good news. He did not believe that the baby had been put in Mary's tummy by God.

He no longer wanted Mary to be his wife.
Mary was very upset.

That night, an angel visited Joseph in his dreams
and told him that the baby really was God's son.
Joseph was to call him Jesus. Joseph was so happy
that he could marry Mary after all.

Many months had passed and the baby was soon to be born. Mary's tummy was large and sore. Joseph told her that the Roman rulers had ordered everyone to travel to their family town to sign their names in a big book. Mary was not happy because they had to go all the way to Bethlehem.

They packed their clothes, strips of cloths for the baby and plenty of food and water. God was with them. He smiled on them all the way.

When Mary and Joseph arrived in Bethlehem it was bustling with visitors. Leaving Mary under the shade of a palm tree, Joseph set off through the crowds to find somewhere to stay. Tired and uncomfortable, Mary waited and watched.

By the time Joseph returned, Mary was crying. So he held her gently and told her about the kind innkeeper who had taken pity on them and offered his stable. At that moment it seemed just perfect.

The stable was bustling with all kinds of animal life.
The bull in the corner huffed and snorted, tossing his
tail this way and that. Little mice scurried and squeaked
in and out of an upturned basket.

With Mary comfortable and the donkey fed and watered,
Joseph looked around their stable home.
Could their baby king really be born in such a poor,
smelly place?

When Jesus was born, Mary was overjoyed.

She scooped him up in her arms and marveled at God's amazing miracle. Wrapping him carefully in strips of cloth, she laid him in a manger to sleep.

On the hillside outside Bethlehem, a group of shepherds sat around a fire, keeping warm. They were loud and rude. They enjoyed being out in the dark where they could do as they pleased.

That night, as the shepherd's laughter rolled about the hilltop, a strange light grew above them. Soon it was shining all around. When the shepherds saw a mighty angel standing in the night sky they were terrified.

'Don't be afraid,' the angel told them. I have great news to tell you. A king has been born, he is called Jesus. This is what you should look for, a baby wrapped in strips of cloth, lying in a manger.' The sky seemed to explode as a host of angels began swooping and singing, 'Glory to God in the highest, and peace on earth to men and women, the ones God loves.'

The light was fading now and the songs were no more than a whisper. The shepherds helped each other to their feet. They began to stumble, then walk, and then run towards the village.

'God's eyes are on me!' shouted one of the shepherds, 'God is with us!' sang another. As they ran, they began to laugh. Joy bubbled inside them like a mountain stream.

They found the stable where Jesus lay and as they walked through the door they were overwhelmed. There was Jesus, their king. They fell to their knees and worshipped him. Jesus would give them a new start. He had turned their darkness into light.

It was still night when the shepherds left the stable. But they did not leave quietly. As they sang, Bethlehem woke from its sleep. Leaning out of windows and standing in doorways, people heard the 'good news' about Jesus and shared the shepherds' joy.

A few weeks later, Mary and Joseph took Jesus to visit the temple in Jerusalem.

An old man called Simeon had spent his whole life watching, waiting and praying for God to send his 'light' back into the world. Today God told him he should visit the temple, as something wonderful would be waiting for him.

As Simeon entered the crowded temple courts, he saw
Joseph with a basket containing a gift of two, pure white
doves and Mary standing close by, holding baby Jesus.
As Simeon took the baby and cradled him in his arms,
his heart was bursting with thanks to God.

'Now I have seen with my own eyes the light that will
change the world. At last I can die in peace.'

Simeon warned Mary and Joseph that Jesus' job was
to show people that their lives needed to change and
that this would make some of
them angry. In fact, just by
hearing about his birth,
someone was already
very angry.

King Herod had no idea about Jesus' birth until a group of travelers called the 'wise men' turned up at the palace. 'Where is the baby king?' they asked. 'We saw his star in the East and have come to worship him.'

King Herod was proud and evil. He would not allow some baby to be as important as him. No way! God had spoken about a 'savior' king being born in Bethlehem. Perhaps this baby was the one.

King Herod pushed the wise men out of the palace door and pointed towards Bethlehem. 'Go and search everywhere for the baby' he snarled, 'and when you find him, come back and tell me so that I too can worship him'.

This was untrue of course. What he planned to do was much worse.

The star went ahead of the wise men and came to rest over a scruffy little house on the outskirts of Bethlehem. The wise men looked out of place in their beautiful, rainbow coloured clothes. Still they gladly knelt down and worshipped the baby.

Opening their treasure box, they presented baby Jesus with gifts of gold, frankincense and myrrh. Each gift was like a story, telling something about who Jesus was, and what he would do.

Gold was a costly gift, fit for a king. Jesus the King! What a lovely present.

Frankincense was a sweet smelling perfume used to worship God.
Jesus was God's Son! How clever of the wise men.

But myrrh? This was a spice used to get people ready for burial!
Did the wise men really want Mary and Joseph to think about Jesus dying?

As the wise men slept that night, they were warned in a dream not to return to Herod's palace. Their lives were in danger and they must travel home by a secret route.

When Herod realised that the wise men were not coming back to the palace to tell him where Jesus could be found, he was furious. They had tricked him. In his madness he gave orders to kill every boy child in Bethlehem under two years old.

'Get up' said the angel to Joseph in a dream.
'Take Jesus and his mother and escape to Egypt.
Stay there until I tell you to leave, because
Herod wants to kill the child'.

Joseph, Mary and Jesus found safety in Egypt.
There they lived, safe in God's hands, until Herod died.
Then God's angel appeared to Joseph once more in
a dream, saying, 'Herod is dead. It's time to go home'.

Our Christmas journey has come to an end.
Mary and Joseph began life as an ordinary little family,
working, eating and playing. Angels no longer talked
to them in their dreams and strange visitors did not
pass by to worship Jesus.

In her heart, Mary remembered all the wonderful things
that happened to Jesus and all that was said about him.
There would be many difficult times ahead, but Mary
would always remind herself that Jesus was God's gift
to the world.

And what a wonderful gift he is. There is so much to be enjoyed at Christmas, but when all the tree lights have been taken down and the parties have ended, Jesus will still be there, showing us God's love and his amazing light.

Thank you Jesus.

GLOSSARY

ANGEL
a messenger from God

BETHLEHEM
the town where Jesus was born

BLESS
make someone happy, give them a gift or help them

CREATION
when God made the world

GABRIEL
an angel sent by God to tell Zechariah and also Mary about having a son

GARDEN OF EDEN
the place which God made for Adam and Eve to live in

HEAVEN
God's special place where everything is perfect

IMMANUEL
a name which means 'God with us'

ISAIAH
a man who had a special message from God about Jesus. He told it to people more than 700 years before Jesus was born

JERUSALEM
the most important city near to where Jesus lived

JOHN	*John the Baptist. Zechariah and Elizabeth were his parents*
MANGER	*where hay was put for the animals to eat*
MIRACLE	*when God does something in an amazing or unexpected way*
NAZARETH	*the town where Joseph and Mary lived. Jesus lived here until he was about 30 years old*
PRIEST	*someone who helped people to worship God*
ROMAN RULERS	*the Romans ruled the country which Jesus lived in*
SAVIOR	*someone who rescues people*
SPIRIT OF GOD	*the way God works in the world*
TEMPLE	*a building where people went to worship God*
WORSHIP	*the way we let God know how much we love him and say thank you for what he has done*

A CHRISTMAS JOURNEY

Copyright ©2001 Susie Poole

Published by Authentic

9 Holdom Avenue, Bletchley, Milton Keynes, Bucks, MK1 1QR,

United Kingdom.

First published 2001 by Word Publishing,

Produced for Authentic by Pupfish Limited.
www.pupfish.co.uk

ISBN: 1-86024-273-1

Printed in China

Authentic